GRIEF

LIAM & PRECIOUS ATCHISON

Dr. Tom Varney
Series Editor

.

NAVPRESS ●

BRINGING TRUTH TO LIFE
NavPress Publishing Group
P.O. Box 35001, Colorado Springs, Colorado 80935

The Navigators is an international Christian organization. Jesus Christ gave His followers the Great Commission to go and make disciples (Matthew 28:19). The aim of The Navigators is to help fulfill that commission by multiplying laborers for Christ in every nation.

NavPress is the publishing ministry of The Navigators. NavPress publications are tools to help Christians grow. Although publications alone cannot make disciples or change lives, they can help believers learn biblical discipleship, and apply what they learn to their lives and ministries.

Some of the anecdotal illustrations in this book are true to life and are included with the permission of the persons involved. All other illustrations are composites of real situations, and any resemblance to people living or dead is coincidental.

Printed in the United States of America

FOR A FREE CATALOG OF
NAVPRESS BOOKS & BIBLE STUDIES,
CALL 1-800-366-7788 (USA)
or 1-416-499-4615 (CANADA)

CONTENTS

FOREWORD

਍

There is one thing missing in this short guide: the authors share very little of their own struggle with grief. A brief reference to Precious Atchison's life-threatening illness is the only window they open into their dark room of trauma and loss.

But perhaps it's better that way. A book with only a little self-disclosure achieves a different purpose than one with a lot. There are two kinds of books on grief. The first invites us into the heart of one who has suffered in order to help us realize that we are not alone. More importantly, it describes a personal journey through grief toward deepening maturity in a way that encourages others to embark on a similar trip. No book of this kind is in the same class as *A Grief Observed* by C. S. Lewis.

The second type of book on grief, like the first, can be written only someone whose soul has been torn apart by tragic loss, but its focus is different. Rather than disclosing personal experience, it addresses the unanswerable questions that grief always surfaces in honest hearts. It seeks to give godly perspective to those who grieve and to those who want to provide comfort.

Each kind of book has its own unique risk. Reports of personal experience with loss sometimes remain on the level of empty-minded sentimentality and never

5

descend into the profound anguish of spirit that sharpens one's awareness of truth. Lewis never makes that mistake.

In books that *discuss* grief rather than *give testimony* about it, unanswerable questions tend to be reduced to merely difficult ones, and then answered. The result can be a collection of impotent truisms that only make the griever feel guilty for not being helped by them.

The Atchisons never fall into this trap. They steer clear of truisms by frankly admitting that the struggle with loss cannot be rearranged into a well-marked path toward resolution. With a sensitivity that can only come out of their own journey through grief, Liam and Precious wisely and gently lead us into the valley of confusion that loss *must* create by stripping away our hopes for an easily explained and manageable world and by refusing to let us retreat into the comfort of arrogant cynicism.

When my brother died in a plane crash, an older man who had earlier lost his adult son spoke at the memorial service. With the passion of ongoing grief and determined hope, he looked into the eyes of our grieving family and said, "Don't be afraid to ask the hard questions. You may not find answers, but you will find God. God reveals Himself to people who have the courage to fully enter their confusion and heartache."

This guide richly expresses the timeless wisdom in that man's comment. It is a powerful reminder to me that grief introduces us to a realm of truth we can find no other way, and it calls us to the kind of love that will keep us faithful until we reach the land where sorrow is not allowed.

Whether you are grieving or seeking to comfort someone who is, read these two books: *A Grief Observed* by C. S. Lewis and *Grief* by Liam and Precious Atchison.

— LARRY CRABB, JR.

INTRODUCTION

ॐ

"Are you in pain, Frodo?" said Gandalf quietly as
he rode by Frodo's side.
        "Well, yes I am," said Frodo. "It is my shoul-
der. The wound aches and the memory of darkness is heavy on me. It was a year ago today."
        "Alas! there are some wounds that cannot be
wholly cured," said Gandalf.
        "I fear it may be so with mine," said Frodo.
"There is no real going back. Though I may come
to the Shire, it will not seem the same; for I shall
not be the same. I am wounded with knife, sting,
and tooth, and a long burden. Where shall I find
rest?"
        Gandalf did not answer.
                —J. R. R. Tolkien, *The Return of the King*

Who would walk into a store and, while surrounded by multitudes of books, stop to look, to touch,
and to open a book on grief? Maybe you are a weary
parent, grasping for a sense of purpose after suffering
the jagged wound of burying your child. Perhaps you
are a lonely griever, your wedding vows dissolved by
death or divorce. Or you have lost a relative or friend:
aunt, uncle, grandparent, brother, sister, parent, neigh-
bor, or mentor. Many of us either have endured the loss

of a parent or are seeing inevitable mortality in the weariness of aging mothers and fathers. Everyone faces it; no one is sure how to handle it. Someone invaded your heart, and now their absence leaves an irreplaceable imprint. Like Frodo, you are not the same and you desperately long for rest.

You are also aware of the sense of powerlessness that occurs when someone in your world suffers a significant loss, and you would like to know what it means to comfort the brokenhearted. Perhaps you identify with Gandalf and fall silent in the presence of deep sorrow.

All who live in this sinful world share a deeply felt pain from disappointment and loss: a severed relationship with "irreconcilable differences"; wounds from abuse, neglect, abandonment; dreams and longings left tightly sealed for fear of rejection, indifference, or even hatred; family members alienated from one another; friends who no longer speak to each other; congregations and church leaders who harshly judge; jobs with no guarantees.

Frankly, we don't do well with loss. We tend to become paralyzed in our anger and resentment, immobilized by despair in the face of seeming injustice. Our ears become deaf, and our hearts grow cold. The deep mystery of the gospel does not break through to us as we dutifully dress up for another Sunday morning. Our smiles mask a breaking heart, and our fine clothes hide our oozing wounds.

To understand losses, we need to be willing to look death in the face. We need to see its intrusive violation of our design for permanent relationships. We need to ask some very difficult questions, beginning with questions of the goodness of God, who we thought would spare us from such intolerable pain. To that end, this discussion guide is not a typical book on grief. There are no detailed discussions of the grief stages, few techniques, and only a promise for a time of future culmination that may lie beyond our deaths. In reality this guide is about the philosophy of living in a sinful world where we must continually face loss and are called upon to choose courageously to look death in the face. We will primarily consider examples that come from death loss, and make applications to other kinds of losses that have caused relational pain.

USING THIS GUIDE

This guide can be used in any one of three ways: (1) on your own; (2) with a group after prior preparation at home; or (3) with a group with no prior preparation. It's amazing how another person's story can spark insights into our own situation. A discussion group shouldn't get larger than twelve people, and four to eight is ideal. If your group is larger than eight, one way to be sure everyone gets plenty of time to talk is to divide into subgroups of four to discuss. This approach can accommodate even a large Sunday school class.

You'll get the most out of the guide if you use both prior preparation and group discussion. Group members can read the text of a session and reflect on the questions during the week. They might keep a journal handy to jot down thoughts, feelings, and questions to bring to the group time. This approach allows time for participants to recall and reflect upon incidents in their lives.

However, a group can also approach the sessions "cold" by reading the text aloud and answering the questions together. If busy schedules make homework impractical, feel free to take this approach.

Finally, if you're using this guide on your own, you'll probably want to record your responses in a journal.

The guide is designed to be covered in six group sessions of sixty to ninety minutes each. However, you could spend a lot more time on some questions. If you have plenty of time, you may want to travel through the guide at your group's own speed.

The sessions contain the following elements:

Text. You'll find words of insight into the topic in each session. Sometimes the text appears all in one chunk; at other times questions fall between blocks of text. You'll probably want someone (or several people) to read the text aloud while the others follow along. Alternatively, you could take a few minutes for each participant to read it silently. If you've all read the text at home, you can of course skip reading it again.

Discussion questions. These will help you understand what you've read and consider how it relates to your own experience and struggles. Each participant's stories will shed light on what the others are going through.

When the text is broken into two or more sections, with questions in between, you should discuss the questions before going on to the next section of text.

Many questions ask participants to talk about themselves. Everyone should feel free to answer at his or her own level of comfort. People will often feel some discomfort if a group is really dealing honestly with issues. However, participants should not feel pressured to talk more personally than they wish. As you get to know each other better, you'll be able to talk more freely.

Prayer. Ideas for closing prayer are offered as suggestions. You may already have a format for praying in your group, or you may prefer not to pray as a group. Feel free to ignore or adapt these ideas.

During the week. In this section you'll find ideas for trying what you've learned and for observing your daily behavior more closely. Feel free to do something else that seems more helpful.

Process notes. The boxed instructions will help the leader keep the group running smoothly. There are also leader's notes at the end of this guide.

FOR MORE BACKGROUND

Whether you're a group leader or a participant, or using this guide on your own, you'll find it helpful to read the introduction to this series from the Institute of Biblical Counseling (IBC): *Who We Are and How We Relate* by Dr. Larry Crabb. It explains the approach to personal growth taught at IBC—the reasoning behind this series' approach to handling problems.

THE COURAGE TO TRAVEL TO THE MORAL FRONTIER

ح∙

LEADER: Introduce yourselves if you don't already know each other. Then ask someone to read the following story aloud.

THE CRAZY, WHITE-HAIRED LADY

There she was again. The "crazy" lady, dressed only in a bathrobe, was tearing the bark off the tree in our front yard. I (Precious) had opportunities to witness many of life's tragedies as I grew up in a parsonage, but this was one of the most extreme I remember. Through my childish eyes I saw only a crazy, white-haired lady, inappropriately dressed and talking loudly to herself. I giggled at her odd ritual, but my pastor-father was serious. "I think you'd better take Mrs. Edwards home," he said to my mother. Years later I heard her story and understood in a very small way the choice Mrs. Edwards made not to feel, not to be, rather only to dance to the music of rage that death had orchestrated.

Before the circumstances that caused Mrs. Edwards to make this choice, people who knew the Edwards family would have described them as happy and well adjusted. The parents and their two sons were very

11

active in church. Mrs. Edwards was a faithful Sunday school teacher, participated in Tuesday afternoon church visitation, and was involved with the women's missionary groups. She was a very proper woman, always neatly dressed, and was admired as a wonderful wife and mother. But one tragic Christmas the Edwards' placid world was shattered.

It was Christmas day and the Edwards family was apart for the first time. The oldest son was in boot camp halfway across the country. Mrs. Edwards decided to take a train to the coast as a holiday surprise for her oldest son. That way, she figured, each son would have a parent with whom they could enjoy the holiday. Her teenage son, Caleb, complained about her proposal when she presented it at the breakfast table one cold December morning. It was bad enough that his brother would be absent. To him it was worse to think that Mom would be gone too. In spite of his protests, the trip was all set. As she boarded the train, Caleb's parting words were, "Christmas won't be the same without you, Mom."

My family was in the middle of opening Christmas packages when Mr. Edwards came to the door. His face was ashen, and he could barely speak. Caleb had been killed in a horrible accident that morning. His parents had thought that the gift of a new motorcycle would soften the disappointment of not being together as a family. In his youthful, reckless excitement he ran a stop sign and never saw the car coming. He was struck and instantly killed.

My father went with Mr. Edwards two days later to meet the train. As Mrs. Edwards walked into the station her first words were, "If only I had been here, this never would have happened." From that moment on, her consuming goal was to avenge her son's death. She lashed out at herself, God, and those she loved the most. Within two years her husband divorced her. She gave away everything she owned. She began to ignore her appearance. There was no joy in life. As the lights of her soul dimmed, it became apparent that Christmas would never again be celebrated. Soon, she became a nuisance to her neighbors, and an urban myth grew around this unkempt woman who reigned as the town oddity, talking to herself and roaming the streets in her bathrobe.

1. In what ways could you explain Mrs. Edwards' behavior as "understandable" given the tremendous pressures she was under?

2. What factors in Mrs. Edwards' life are similar to those in your own life?

LEADER: Remind the group on question 3 that having Mrs. Edwards in a small group before the tragedy is hypothetical. It is abstract to say that there might be things the church could teach to equip us to handle tragedy. There is no proof that more education better prepares us to handle life's problems. The question can be used as a comparison to explain how we anticipate dealing with tragedy.

3. If Mrs. Edwards had been in a small-group study you were leading before the accident, what would you have liked to tell her that might have better prepared her for her son's death?

LEADER: The next section deals with how death is part of a picture that is very different from God's ideal for people. Answer question 4 and examine the scripture verses before reading the section "A Violation of the Rules." You may want to have a different person read each question. The context of Genesis 1–3 may not be familiar to everyone, so help group members to understand. Also help them see how these passages fit into the message of the entire book of Genesis. Some have suggested that the message of Genesis is, "God keeps His promises." If anyone doubts that God indeed kept His promises to Adam, he or she should read Genesis 5. The focus is not on the long life spans, but on the oft-repeated "and he died."

4. Look up the following passages one at a time, and put together a list of items that describe God's original design for people.

   a. Read Genesis 1:26–2:3. Particularly note what people are and what God intended for them to do.

   b. Read Genesis 2:15-25. How important and permanent were relationships intended to be?

c. Read Genesis 3:1-24. Contrast the characteristics of God's ideal design for people with the changes that resulted when the man and woman sinned.

REFLECTION

We are often disappointed even in the best of relationships. Mourners sometimes feel guilty for past words and actions that fell short of loving. However, to be in relationship with someone means to risk being hurt by the sins and failures of others. Sometimes in grief the pain of what never existed in the relationship, and now will never be on this earth, is even greater than the grief over what actually was.

5. a. What did you want most from the relationship you are grieving?

   b. What would you have wanted to be different?

   c. If you could, what would you want to tell the person whose loss you are grieving?

15

d. What do you miss most about the person you are
grieving? What do you not miss?

A VIOLATION OF THE RULES

The example of Mrs. Edwards may seem extreme. In
fact many grief counselors would describe this tragic
story as an abnormal grief reaction, a pathological dis-
order. Yet there is something in Mrs. Edwards' horrid
experience that requires us not to dismiss her actions as
merely extraordinary behavior.

She could have adopted the spiritual platitudes
that were possibly offered by those who attempted to
comfort her. She might have resigned herself to the
hollow comfort of words like, "Think how happy Caleb
must be in Heaven," or "He's in a better place," or
"God must have a purpose for this." Even adopting the
self-searching suggestion of a blatantly cruel and all
too common remark like, "What sin in your life caused
this to happen?" would seem to have been better than
choosing to resign from the human race.

Instead, Mrs. Edwards acted out her drama of rage
in her pastor's front yard, a man who represented God
to her. Her script proclaimed the violation of God's
design for her. Beyond the wild hair and hollow eyes
of her appearance, her manner preached a sermon that
few heard, and yet its thesis should be familiar to all
who are thoughtful about death and grief. In fact, her
behavior is understandable in light of the numerous
violations that occurred when her son was killed. Consider some of the "rules" that were broken when the
teen died.

Natural order was violated. It isn't natural for parents
to bury their children. In the rhythm of life two people
get married, have children, enjoy their grandchildren,
and are cared for by children and grandchildren in
their old age. People expect this orderly progression to

16

the grave, but the death of a child upsets the rhythm. Grieving parents usually display anger when a child dies because it isn't natural, it isn't fair. *The rule of reaping and sowing was violated.* Every parent believes that good parents protect their children. Mrs. Edwards had done everything she thought was involved in being a good mother. She made every reasonable provision for Caleb's safety. She believed that the result of her careful consideration would be that he would greet her when she returned on the train. Nevertheless, at the time of his greatest need she was not there. She could not stop the car that struck him.

The rule of relational permanence was violated. People who love each other should always be together. Objectively speaking, one might say that this is unreasonable. People who love each other are often apart, sometimes permanently. We should understand that this is unreasonable only if we were *not* created for everlasting relationships. The creation account in Genesis makes it plain that the man and woman were created for permanent relationship with each other and with God. Later, when Adam sinned, death entered the human drama. Adam and Eve, and all their descendants, were now sinners. However, their fundamental orientation to unending love relationships had never been altered. We are usually sad when we believe it is necessary to end a relationship, but we may become outraged when a relationship is terminated without our permission. The termination violates the fact that we were designed to have resilient, lasting relationships.

The "loving, heavenly Father" rule was violated. God is a loving, heavenly Father who cares for His children. However, He is also all-powerful and present everywhere. Unfortunately, that means He was at the scene of the accident, could have prevented it, but chose not to. In other words, it appears that He chose to stand by and do nothing. That doesn't sound like a loving, heavenly Father. This violation is almost universally observed by grieving people. It is so disturbing that

17

theological explanations fail when comforters attempt to provide them.

6. a. What "rules" were broken at the time of your own loss or at the loss of someone you know?

   b. How did you or the person you know respond to these "violations"?

MEETING OUR MORAL FRONTIER

What is the usual response when the rules are broken? Often it is indignant anger that may lead a person to refuse to think through the violation or recognize the anger. Few of us have instability or blatant nerve like Mrs. Edwards. She refused to survive the death of her son, a loss she unconsciously realized she was never created to face. Yet, how many people who have suffered loss have dimmed the lights of their souls, inwardly dancing to the music of rage, undetected by those around them who have no clue that someone is out in the cold scantily dressed?

Mrs. Edwards' choice to act crazy showed her refusal to allow the injustice of the sinful world system to enter her orderly life. So she acted out this strange logic by tearing bark from her pastor's tree. The alternative would have been to return to her placid, well-regulated life, in spite of what she observed as the absurdity of her spirituality and orderliness. She refused to accept the alternative because the rules she had used to make life work failed.

We often urge grievers to move back to normalcy, back to the rhythms of life as they were before tragedy struck—back to denial of the apparent absurdity of life. In the Christian community, we lack the courage of Solomon, who could say, "Utterly meaningless! Everything is meaningless" (Ecclesiastes 1:2). The griever is very near a basic understanding of truth, but all too often is urged to pull back from thinking about it too deeply. This basic truth is, *this world is broken and we cannot fix it.* Adam and Eve were created to enjoy a world without sweat, without weeds, without pain, without suffering, without death. We are designed like Adam and Eve. The problem is, we have never experienced a world like the Garden of Eden. We were built for it, just as airplanes were built to fly. Instead of flying, we use the plane as a submarine and assume that is the way it is supposed to be. Death is *normal*, it is the norm, because all we know is that people live and then they die; but death is not *natural*, because we were not created to die.

Somewhere in the depths of her soul, Mrs. Edwards understood how absurd it was to accept death as natural and to live life as if the violation of the rules meant nothing. So rather than return to the masquerade of her orderly life, she created a new reality, a parallel world of her own making.

Was Mrs. Edwards' response the correct one? No, because she was unwilling to wrestle with the difficult questions of life. Neither is it correct to hurry on with life as if nothing has changed. We often believe that we can control life and make it work by following a few principles or steps. The problem is, if we could block out all the suffering in the world and be "normal" by some method, technique, or formula, why would we need God? Indeed, we would not need to be redeemed because we could save ourselves. This is the path followed by many who reach for an antidepressant, a seminar, or a how-to book in an effort to find some technique (even a spiritual one) that will make it possible not to have to reckon with a God who stands by when tragedy happens to someone they love.

So what alternative is left when we have to face a devastating loss? What hope is there? Oswald Chambers said that all who face this kind of agony have a rare opportunity:

> Redemption does not amount to anything to a man until he meets an agony; until that time he may have been indifferent; but knock the bottom board out of his wits, bring him to the limit of his moral life, produce the supreme suffering worthy of the name of agony, and he will begin to realize that there is more in redemption than he had ever dreamed, and it is at that phase that he is prepared to hear Jesus Christ say, "Come unto Me. . ." Our Lord said, "I did not come to call the man who is all right; I came to call the man who is at his wit's end, the man who has reached the moral frontier."[1]

We define a moral frontier as *a place, event, or circumstance that causes us to realize our true neediness and reveals our unsuccessful efforts to manage our world.* The griever is at a moral frontier, a crossroad where a decision must be made: "Shall I return to life the way I knew it before my loss, as if this never happened, and attempt to numb the pain by the routines and techniques of 'normal living'? Or, shall I create a world of fantasy where good always triumphs, rules are never broken, and I live happily ever after?" These alternatives divert us from our moral frontier, but are also cowardly because they do not require us to stand in awe and amazement at a Savior who died for sinful people. There is a more courageous option than either denial or withdrawal, but *we must first be convinced of our tendency to refuse to look death in the face.*

7. Consider the definition of a moral frontier. Name a time when you encountered a moral frontier. How did you respond to the circumstance?

STILLNESS

Close the session with conversational prayer. If the content of this session has raised some difficult questions for you, you may want to use the following prayer:

> Lord, it is painfully hard for me to think about Your original design for me, because I am left with a deep, dark, lonely vacuum that nothing on this earth can fill. Still, I know You want me to love You and love others. This is often hard for me. This moral frontier is frightening to me because. . . .

DURING THE WEEK

The following activities will cause you to reflect on the material discussed in this first session. You may choose one of these options, and if you would like, share your results with the group the next time you meet.

- Begin a journal this week in which you make several entries relating your own life's story. You may want to review the text of this session and incorporate some of the descriptive language, such as "moral frontier," "violation," or "relationships," to help tell your story.

- Draw two pictures using colors that visually depict you or someone you know. The first picture would portray life *before* and the second would illustrate life *after* the loss you talked about in question 6.

- Compose a poem about life, describing its joys and disappointments. You may choose to relate it to the loss you talked about in question 6, and you may want to use some of the descriptive language used in this session.

NOTE
1. Oswald Chambers, *The Shadow of an Agony/The Highest Good* (Grand Rapids, MI: Discovery House Publishers, 1992), page 28.

THE COURAGE TO FACE LOSS

ื๕

> LEADER: Members may want to report some
> details about the assigned activities they worked
> on during the week.

THE DISCOMFORT OF GRIEF

She had been asked to read her thoughts on the loss she
had recently experienced. She first offered a tearful dis-
claimer. She was afraid her words might upset someone
in the group. She timidly began to reveal the contents
of her grieving heart. She was a single woman who was
robbed of motherhood when her seventeen-year-old
daughter was killed in a mysterious plane accident. Her
deep loneliness and the despair of being instantly child-
less shook the group. However, tears of sympathy turned
to an uncomfortable silence as she continued to pour out
her heart. She told us of her journey to find hope and her
determined efforts to find God at various churches.

When she told of looking for God at a church with
Bible in its name, I (Precious) began to shift uncomfort-
ably in my seat. She explained that it stood to reason
that because God had written the Bible, He could be
found at a church if the name boldly bore the name

of that book. Instead, she felt out of place in her faded jeans and wrinkled shirt that Sunday morning—everyone else was so dressed up. She figured that was why no one acknowledged her presence there. She continued by recalling the pastor's sermon. His cold and distant words about God and sin left her feeling unworthy, unclean, unfit. She thought he meant that she should come back only when she could disguise her pain through smiles and singing and proper clothes. She ended by saying that she hoped she would actually discover that there is no God. She said it would be harder for her to believe that there indeed is a God who was there the night of her daughter's death, yet chose to be merely a spectator.

When she was finished telling her story, we had a coffee break. I saw that I was not the only uncomfortable one. Several people in the group approached her during the break and tried to convince her that she was somehow missing the point. I felt a strong urge to enter into the theological bantering, but I fell silent. My mind was thinking of how and what questions: *How* could I convince her? *What* should she understand better? *What* should I say in God's defense? But her grief-filled inquiries were in a different category. They were *why* questions. In the anger of mourning, she was asking God why this happened, and further, why things are the way they are. The would-be comforters should have entered into the why category as well. Now really, why did her young daughter have to die on a trip that was meant to result in pleasure and memories? My answer? I don't know why. I'm not God, and He does not make me privy to His sovereign will. He is not completely silent, He speaks in His Word. But the heavens are silent concerning the tragic death of that teenage girl.

1. a. What questions or doubts about your faith make you feel uncomfortable?

24

b. How do you handle those uncomfortable situations?

2. a. List some of your own why questions.

  b. How have you or others tried to answer these questions?

  c. Why do easy answers to difficult questions often fail to satisfy us?

CHOOSING TO FACE THE REALITY OF GRIEF

We must begin our path to healing by looking death in the face regardless of the discomfort or pain it may cause us. It will make us uncomfortable because we cannot hide from it or explain it away by clever argumentation. In the words of Oswald Chambers, loss introduces us to an agony. Agony brittles the bones, wearies the body, and breaks the heart. In our efforts to escape the kind of neediness agony produces, we do our best to hide ourselves and others, patterning our actions after those of Adam and Eve, weaving fig leaves to cover us. We imagine that by doing so we will spare ourselves from discomfort and defend God. However, the refusal to face difficult, perhaps unresolvable, questions and doubts in reality declares that God is not enough and that we have convincing data of His impotence. We instead settle for platitudes that explain God, and we become weary in our attempts to make Him look good in the face of such contradictory evidence.

The courage to look death and loss in the face means asking appropriate questions. There are *why* questions to be asked if I am to understand grief. Many of them arise in the moment of discomfort, and if we are attuned to them, we can gain insight into our futile efforts to banish death and loss from our world. Consider first our impotent efforts to cover over the raw agony of grief. We often deafen our ears to the hard questions that are asked when people find themselves facing tragedy. Why was I uncomfortable as this woman was reprimanding the church and raging at God, who didn't come through for her? Why were various members of the group who confronted her offering "fig leaf" coverings intended to hide her oozing pain? Why can't I believe that God is big enough to endure antagonism and demands that scream, "If you are God, spare us the consequences of sin and blanket us from the effects of the Fall"? Why, in my arrogance, do I see it as my duty to defend God?

Dealing with grief issues presents an opportunity to see clearly what we do with our lives even when we are not grieving: We want to deny, hold back, and even reverse the effects of the Fall *without any help from God.*

Instead, we need to be willing to face the reality of loss by not dodging the difficult questions of grief. This will prepare us to feel the pain of grief. But why should we do that? To feel the pain without a goal in view is only morbidity. We must understand the purpose of the grieving process.

3. Read Genesis 3:7. Why did the man and woman sew fig leaves to cover themselves?

We are using fig leaves to describe the disguises that cover our pain, vulnerability, and true neediness as sinful people. In loss and grief we come closest to seeing the inadequacies of these efforts to disguise. Examples of fig leaves can be—

- Busyness that never allows reflection.
- Poor self-esteem, which demands that no one expect anything from us.
- Fragile overdependence on others that forces them to handle us with special care.
- Tough, hard exteriors that proclaim to the world that we have no need of others.
- Characteristics of the class clown and even the competent CEO who use a style of relating to mask fears and insecurities.
- Our manner when we offer only the mind in a relationship and never the heart.
- People-pleasing strategies calculated to guarantee that others will love and accept us.
- Messiah complexes that cause us to be determined to rescue all those in need around us, because God either needs help or is incapable of action.

4. a. What are some of the fig leaves, coverings, you use to disguise your neediness?

b. What illusions do your fig leaves give to you and to others?

c. What do your fig leaves say about how you view God?

UNDERSTANDING THE GOAL
OF THE GRIEVING PROCESS

Perhaps you selected this guide because you or someone you know has experienced a loss and you would like to learn how to "get back to normal." It certainly seems reasonable to look for help, relief, and hope for a better tomorrow. Yet we wonder, should the goal of the grieving process as well as grappling with life's other problems be to find answers to difficult questions, to be relieved of pain and to recover? Might this goal cause us to miss an important part of the gospel—our neediness, the ongoing necessity of relationship with God, and a loving community with a hope for the future? Is God more interested in our recovery or in our seeking Him in the midst of the mess of life in a broken world?

The goal of the grieving process is not recovery but putting the person who was lost into such an appropriate place in our memory that our hope for the future is intensified, while life on earth is more deeply felt and experienced. This means that the goal of grief is not to forget, but to remember the one lost. Sometimes people are afraid to remember because they fear that others will tire of their grief. Sometimes they fear the pain of remembering. That is why remembrance must be appropriate.

The goal of grieving is to acknowledge four things. First, I must confess what the loss means to me. I will never be the same and neither will my world. Second, I must accept the emotions that accompany the recognition of these profound changes. I may feel anguish, despair, anger, numbness, depression, or confusion. Third, I must face the fact that I have doubts at many levels. I may question what I have really believed about life and God. I shouldn't seek to become angry at God, but I may indeed harbor some doubts and resentment that I have feared to bring into the open. Finally, I need to embrace the mystery of God. This includes the same lesson that Job learned—God's ways are inscrutable. God cannot be controlled; He is not under obligation to explain His ways to us.

Grief that acknowledges and anguishes over the bitter experiences of life will result in a longing for the future. This longing may be for reunion in Heaven with the loved one lost, though each of us has nagging doubts about the eternal destiny of lost loved ones. Looking forward to the future is ultimately longing for God's future: the return of Christ, the termination of death, and the establishment of His justice. This longing does not result in a paralyzed despair, but instead enables grievers to enjoy glimpses of the future, which our good God gives to increase our anticipation. As grievers we will more fully enjoy God's creation and our own unique ability to create. Now, too, we deeply appreciate relationships with God and others. We encounter the greater possibility of richly enjoying God's goodness in spite of being survivors who must remain in a world that groans in anticipation of the day of redemption. Remembrance, then, is essentially anguish and anticipation.

Consider the garden we were built to occupy. Sin had not entered the picture in Eden. As a result, death was unknown. When they sinned, God expelled the man and the woman and locked the gate behind them. From the time the sentence for sin was pronounced, God said a Redeemer was their only hope to recover what was lost in the garden. Oswald Chambers spoke of this when he said, "According to the Bible, the basis of things is tragedy and the way out is the way by God in redemption." He made promises for the future that have not been fulfilled yet, and that is why He calls us to persevere in faith. In the meantime, He shows mercy to the unbeliever in allowing him or her to continue to live with the opportunity of repentance ever an option.

To the believer He provides continual communication and occasional samples of the joy that in the future will be the unending possession of the glorified saints.

However, we grow impatient, or we mistakenly think that a relationship with God is tantamount to an experiential restoration to the garden. We are shocked when tragedy strikes us (and so we should be because we were created to live in a garden of perpetual delight). Then we take matters into our own hands. God needs to be defended. We convince ourselves that we really do live in a garden after all, and all that is needed is to do some weeding. But we don't see that our garden is nothing but weeds; it's only that some weeds are more tolerable to us than others. We especially seek to destroy the weeds that remind us that we do not really live in a garden at all: disappointment, illness, nonorganic depression, and especially grief. We despise grief because it is so closely linked to death. We don't want to think about death—it is so unpleasant and gardens should be pleasant. Indeed, death is a forbidden topic of conversation. Thinking about it is the ultimate in negative thinking. And so, our systems of thinking, awareness of fear, and techniques of acting serve us well as we foolishly attempt to exile death from our lives, and perpetuate the folly by encouraging others to do the same.

An example of this folly is the way many people speak about the bereaved. If the griever keeps a stiff upper lip and doesn't speak of doubting God's goodness, it is often said he or she is "doing well." However, if the bereaved wail, carry on, and rebuff sensible theological arguments we say they are not doing well at all. Such pervasive thinking on the part of would-be comforters is just as well-intended as Peter's efforts to keep Jesus from going to the cross—and almost as sinister. We must allow the mourner to experience the real emotions that God designed for the expatriated garden-dweller. Loss reminds us that we continue to live in a sinful world that can be fixed only in the good time of the One who will redeem it.

In the meantime, we must realistically face our disappointment in being banished from the garden and give up our efforts to recover it in our time frame. We need to move, however feebly, to the kind of faith spoken of by the author of Hebrews, a faith that God will keep His promises in the future even though we presently experience heartache, sorrow, and death. But first we must mourn with the deep, heaving sighs of those who are pilgrims in a strange country where they don't belong. Those who would comfort must be silent in the presence of the mourner — even when he or she questions God — because in reality, the mourner senses the heart of God. In relationship to His creation, He is, above all, a mourning lover. That is why He draws our hope to the future and blesses the mourner so close to His heart by saying, "Blessed are those who mourn, for they will be comforted" (Matthew 5:4).

5. How does the truth that you were never created to face such a loss affect you? (Is it a relief or a source of frustration?) Explain.

6. In light of the previous discussion, what do you think would be some appropriate goals of the grieving process? Remember that appropriate grieving should result in an intensified hope for the future.

ASPECTS OF THE GRIEF PROCESS

What is the biblical approach to living in a world where sin and death persist? The entire Bible was given to help the sojourning pilgrim answer this question, but here are four main observations.

First, *we should recognize that grief is inevitable, and we must courageously choose to walk through our doubts, fears, and depression.* Though grief is not pleasant, it changes our lives forever. If we do not walk through its wilderness, we will not learn the wonder of dependence on God, we will miss the opportunity of taking a risk to trust Him in the midst of the absurdity that surrounds us. We should be willing to walk through grief when we experience loss, but we may prepare for the inevitable day of grieving by allowing others who are experiencing grief to walk through it.

Have you found that you quickly rejoice with those who celebrate yet hesitate to weep with those who cry? Could this natural, effortless response toward happy events reveal consonance with what you were created for? Does the uncomfortable, impotent feeling we experience around someone, for example, who has just lost a spouse, reveal a dissonance of the design? Somehow death forces us to look upon something that we cannot manage, cannot control, and requires something of us that we do not inherently possess. Why would we want to comfort the empty-armed mother whose son was stillborn by saying that miscarriages are God's way of intervening in an unhealthy pregnancy? Remarks like this are attempts to shrink the overwhelming pain into reasonable, manageable levels that will not require us to agonize over the actual earthly loss.

We must stop giving scripture verses to the grieving as a Valium to numb the pain, to control the confusion, to manage the unmanageable.

Second, *we should understand that God is big enough to handle rage and doubts.* To borrow from Luther's thoughts about God's Word, we should realize that He is a lion, and no one defends a lion. When we become uncomfortable in the presence of the doubts of others, it is often because we smother our own doubts about a faith that may not really be our own. Our faith in God cannot be the faith of our parents, pastors, theologians, favorite authors, or seminary professors. It must be our own. Thinking seriously about life affords us the opportunity to choose to make our faith our own. Above all we should not withdraw from those who doubt in the midst of their grief. C. S. Lewis observed that people are disturbed by the presence of the griever:

> An odd by product of my loss is that I'm aware of being an embarrassment to everyone I meet. At work, at the club, in the street, I see people as they approach me, trying to make up their minds whether they'll say something or not. I hate it if they do and if they don't. I like best the well brought up young men who walk up to me as if I were a dentist, turn very red, get it over and then edge away to the bar as quickly as they decently can. Perhaps the bereaved ought to be isolated in special settlements like lepers.[1]

Third, *we must realize that God wants us to recognize our neediness.* We need God and we need other people as we live in a broken world of ever-encroaching evil. We will never recover, in the sense of regaining what was lost in the garden, until Christ returns. For now, God wants us to move toward a trust in Him that will enable us to remain in life's race and finish well. We must also recognize that we do not run the race alone: "Let us consider how we may spur one another on toward love and good deeds" (Hebrews 10:24). In a later session, we will discuss the necessity of moving toward other people in a way that does not give false hope. This leads to the last observation.

Fourth, *we are to embrace hope for the future that God has prepared for us.* It is a real hope that, properly understood, offers a reason to go on living. The goal of the grieving process is not recovery but remembering the person who was lost in an appropriate way so that our hope for the future is intensified. We are to remember the tokens of Heaven, such as loved ones who were dear to us, because they remind us of our pilgrim status on earth and point us to the future when God will fulfill His promises.

Meanwhile, how do we continue to live in a sinful world as we bear the wounds of our loss?

> LEADER: Encourage each person in the group to close silently with the following prayer.

STILLNESS

Lord, it is winter in my life. In my loss I have begun to exhaust what I never expected would be limited: my own strength to cope. Others view me as . . . , yet I feel. . . . I know I cover my own pain with . . . because the rawness of agony feels. . . . Lord, the leaves that I search for to hide my vulnerability from You and others seem scarce, and I am left feeling painfully exposed.

> LEADER: Members should feel the freedom not to share the results of the following *optional* activity with the group.

DURING THE WEEK

In a notebook or journal, chart your pilgrimage since your loss. Feel free to structure the chart any way you wish. It should be a list of significant events, little encouragements, or setbacks that you believe define your loss in an important way. Be sure to include an account of the emotions that have accompanied you on your journey.

NOTE
   1. C.S. Lewis, *A Grief Observed* (New York: Bantam Books, 1976), pages 10-11.

THE COURAGE TO HOPE

ۮ

LEADER: Ask for a volunteer to read the following story.

CHOOSING TO LIVE

I can't begin to explain what I've been through in the last two weeks. I've had guilt, anger, and loneliness all wrapped together. What a wild roller coaster! Grief is a funny thing. About the time you think you've got it together, grief sweeps over you like a tidal wave. When you lose a spouse to death there are so many adjustments to make. Sometimes simple things seem like mountains. There are days when confidence disappears and deciding what to cook for dinner is impossible. There are days when coming home is painful. There are times when I wonder at my ability to parent and nights when the bed is so cold. There are days when I say, "God, are You sure You know what You're doing?" I know He knows and doesn't make mistakes. And to make matters worse, someone will say, "You are doing so well,"

35

and "You are doing so well with the boys," and
"You're so stable." I think, *If you only knew*. By
the grace of God, I've become secure in how very
much God loves me, and with that knowledge
I can face whatever I need to and I can go on
with life.

This reflection came from the letter of a young
mother of three who lost her husband about eight-
een months before she penned these thoughts. She
confronted the reality of loss and concluded, "I will
never be the same again, but I will choose to live." The
courage to hope demonstrated in this letter draws us
and causes us to marvel at the grace of God that has
given her a very simple truth of which to be absolutely
convinced: God loves me. The well-meaning comforter
often seeks to marshal complex theological arguments
in his or her self-protective attempts to defend God's
wisdom in allowing the loss. God's grace is so powerful
when it is attested to in the profoundly simple affirma-
tion of His love by a survivor who perhaps only days or
moments before stood in the place of the angry doubter.

1. The love of God was an anchor for the young widow
   whose thoughts we just witnessed. What are some
   anchors that ground you in the storms of your
   losses?

THREE COURAGEOUS QUESTIONS

The very existence of grief—whether personally experienced or observed from a distance—should invite
us to wonder what the essentials of the faith are. At
least three questions must be considered in light of
devastating loss. We state them here more formally than
a person in the depths of loss would state them.

- Are the formulas that I believed would lead to a happy life really valid?

- Why am I angry and depressed when I see life going on around me as if nothing happened?

- Did God allow this to happen for some purpose, or is this loss as meaningless as it seems? Another way to ask this is, Is there any hope?

We will consider each of these questions in an effort to understand the courage to hope we saw demonstrated in the letter of the mother of three.

Are the Formulas that I Believed Would Lead to a Happy Life Really Valid?

In session 1 we mentioned Mrs. Edwards' stable Christian lifestyle prior to the death of her son. Still, for all the outward appearances, Mrs. Edwards' philosophy of life did not sustain her when the chips were down. Most of us can think of people who surprised us by turning away from God during a difficult time. Perhaps we were shocked when we heard of a well-known pastor who had been carrying on an affair for years without missing a step in the pulpit. Ugly emotions that emerge from our own lives from time to time cause us to wonder if God is really at work in us. We can raise many questions about these instances but the most common one is, "What went wrong?" In a moment of weakness a choice was made, and we assume the choosers swerved from the path they were on. But what if they really did not swerve? What if the bad choices we often make are not divergent at all? What if they were choices *perfectly consistent with the formulas that work for us*?

Most of us are rationalists to the core. A rationalist believes that all truth can be obtained through right thinking. Believing in God becomes logical. When the bereaved doubts God's existence we become uncomfortable. We often believe that we can follow certain steps and guarantee health and happiness. Even faith becomes rational—the more faith we pour on, the better the outcome. If we are depressed, we simply follow a series of steps to cure it: take a cold shower, go jogging, alter our diet, memorize a verse, do something selfless. To approach life and our problems in this way denies the mystery of existence. Experiencing depression, for example, is an opportunity to desire relationship with God and stand in awe at the mystery of Him. Instead, we don't need God when we have a sure-fire formula to beat depression. And to make our formulas more spiritual, we may throw in prayer and Bible memory—who on earth would ever argue with that?

Rationalism is an attempt to obligate God to my agenda. If I am a good parent then my kids must turn out as successful and spiritual adults. If I tithe then God must bless my business. If I care for my family then my spouse must be faithful to me. But tragedy is not rational, death is not rational. It messes up all our neat formulas and categories. When death touches me too closely I am miffed at God for not doing what I thought I had obligated Him to do.

When our formula does not work we are presented with an opportunity: We can either approach God's throne of grace to find help and mercy in our time of need (Hebrews 4:16), or we can go searching for a new formula. Some of us spend our entire lives moving from one formula and one seminar to another formula and another seminar. Like drug addicts who get enough to make it one more day, we weep with joy when we are blessed with one more formula to replace the one that didn't work anymore.

Grief allows us to examine our formulas. When the young mother wrote about her grief, she did not proclaim that all her formulas worked or that the experience showed her a series of principles that were the key to life. The thing that she clung to was very simple: "God loves me." Sufferers are not comforted by steps or theological principles. Comfort did not come to the Old Testament character of Job through the explanations of his friends. Comfort came when God showed His

38

strength in the leviathan that could not be tamed. My response to the God of mystery is to wonder at His love.

Why Am I Angry and Depressed When I See Life Going on Around Me as If Nothing Happened?

Grief causes us to look more accurately at our disappointments and longings. The world is moving on in denial of death, as if death were not awaiting all of us. The bereaved person perceives the reality of life's situation. Death, suffering, and/or loss await all of us. Each loss is a reminder of what each of us will eventually face. It is as John Donne said, "Ask not for whom the bell tolls, it tolls for thee."

However, inevitability does not mean that loss is natural. Hurt and depression accompany grief because our longings for relationship have been disappointed. When a beloved husband dies before his time, his wife becomes depressed because she had longed to share old age with him. When a daughter dies in youth, her father grieves because he longs for the relationship that once was and the grandchildren that will never be. The widow grieves because she longed never to be lonely; relationships were never intended to end. When the beloved is buried dreams may be buried with him.

Anger and depression are the results of deep disappointments of which our losses remind us. We were created for a garden where there was no death or suffering. Loss is a reminder that the man and the woman were turned out of that garden. We yearn for the permanence and fulfillment of relationships that was lost when Adam sinned. Is there any hope for us?

Did God Allow This to Happen for Some Purpose, Or Is This Loss as Meaningless as It Seems?

One man who had lost two children said, "I ask God to tell me why this happened. I feel I could accept it if He would just give me a good reason. I pray and pray but the heavens are silent."

When we hear this kind of anguish we often try to come up with some answer: "Perhaps you will be allowed to help someone who experiences a similar loss." "Maybe God wanted to teach you to value His love more than theirs." "God may use this to draw your unsaved relatives to Him." Sometimes the explanations people offer are inane: "God took her because He wanted another angel in Heaven." This last statement assumes the Lord of the universe could need her more than you do. The heavens may be silent, but theology is not useless. There should be a strong sense of the "not yet" in our theology. That is, we must remember that the answers to our most important questions will not be given until we are with Christ.

Suffering and loss are for today, but resurrection and restoration are for the future. Mourning is appropriate because the pain of my present loss of relationship feels greater than the eternal hope promised by Christ's resurrection. Acceptance after a time of mourning does not mean getting back to the everyday methods of denial; instead, it means finally embracing the hope of the resurrection. Tim Hansel relates a story from his pastor that shows the wisdom of children to grasp the hope of the resurrection:

> It was a story about Johnny, a young boy who had a terminal disease and not long to live. His disease made it very difficult for him to understand classroom assignments. During the Easter season, the children were supposed to take an empty "Easter egg" (actually a L'eggs panty hose container) and put something in it that reminded them of life and of Easter.
>
> The day the eggs were turned in, the teacher opened each one in turn and made a positive comment on what each child had put inside. Observing that one egg was empty, she assumed that it was Johnny's and that, as usual, he didn't understand the assignment.
>
> When she finished, Johnny raised his hand and said, "But Teacher, you didn't share mine."
>
> "I'm sorry, Johnny, but you didn't under-

stand. You were to bring something that means Easter to you, that represents life, and put it into the egg."

"But Teacher," Johnny said, "Jesus' tomb was empty—and that is what life is really all about."

Johnny died a few weeks later, and in his casket his classmates placed twenty-seven empty eggs. They understood.

He is risen; He is risen; He is risen indeed. His empty tomb means our hearts can be full.[1]

The resurrection is a token, a sample of Christ's eventual victory over the enemies that plague me in a sinful world. As Nicholas Wolterstorff said, "I shall look at the world through tears. Perhaps I will see things that dry-eyed I could not see." So I will live as a mourner who struggles with the unfinished program of God and long for the day when there will be no death, mourning, crying, or pain, and sorrow and sighing shall flee away:

> Then I saw a new heaven and a new earth, for the first heaven and the first earth had passed away, and there was no longer any sea. I saw the Holy City, the new Jerusalem, coming down out of heaven from God, prepared as a bride beautifully dressed for her husband.
>
> And I heard a loud voice from the throne saying, "Now the dwelling of God is with men, and he will live with them. They will be his people, and God himself will be with them and be their God. He will wipe every tear from their eyes. There will be no more death or mourning or crying or pain, for the old order of things has passed away." (Revelation 21:1-4)

2. What formulas that you were sure would work failed you in a difficult time? What formulas have been shaken since you began the first session of this study? (A formula often runs like this: "If I just . . .

41

then God will. . . ." For example, "If I just faithfully pray for my children, then God will keep them safe from harm.")

3. What are some questions about life or loss that you would like God to answer when you get to Heaven?

4. a. Describe a story from your life about a deeply disappointing experience.

   b. How might the feelings of disappointment that were highlighted by the event find fulfillment in the eternal future God has planned?

STILLNESS

Lord, in the midst of the pain and confusion of my loss I believe You are. . . . Ease my fear of Your mystery and silence, and help me to anticipate in deeper ways the day when the pain of . . . caused by my loss will be no more.

LEADER: The purpose of the following word-picture exercise is to give group members an opportunity to be a creative part of their grief and hope. Without metaphors, we often relate to our experiences as if they never really happened to us. Our hope in Christ is not just a theological fact but a reality to be embraced. Word pictures enable us to express that reality in a way that touches our own hearts and gives others a meaningful glimpse into our suffering, and into what God has provided for us in the midst of that suffering.

DURING THE WEEK

Write a sentence or two that uses a word picture, parable, metaphor, or simile to describe how your loss and your hope for the future make you feel. For example, "I felt like I was going against the current in a flash flood, fighting against being swept away, and then, suddenly, I landed on a rock and felt secure as the waters continued to swirl around me." The psalmists often used word pictures to convey grief and hope. You may want to find a word picture in the psalms, if you can identify with the experience and insight.

NOTE
1. Tim Hansel, *Through the Wilderness of Loneliness* (Elgin, IL: David C. Cook Publishing Co., 1991), pages 80-81.

THE COURAGE TO LOVE AND GIVE

≥▲

LEADER: This session is designed to cause group members to examine the world views that influence people and affect their ability to grieve and to move beyond their disappointments. You may want to begin the session by asking someone to read aloud the following story.

LIFE IS LIKE A TUNNEL

Like many people who live near the Rockies, our family always enjoys a ride in the mountains. If you were to ask our children what they remember most about our drives in the high country, they would probably mention going through one of the many tunnels marvelously cut straight through solid rock. The reason they will remember this is not because the tunnels demonstrate the genius of human engineering, but because of a silly travel custom we have passed on to the kids from our own childhood. No one in our family is sure how the tradition got started, but whenever we enter a tunnel, we have a contest to see who can hold his or her breath the entire way through. Short tunnels are easy; but the longer the tunnel. . . . Though it takes only a moment or two to pass through the long tunnels, when you are holding your breath it seems like forever.

The tunnel experience gives a picture of what life on earth is like. As in the tunnel, life on earth is relatively dark and shadowy. We move rapidly through the hole and feel that it is intolerable as we hold our breath. We feel as if we can't stand it any longer, when in reality we are only seconds into the darkness. Because we do not breathe as freely as God intended, it seems as if passing through the tunnel takes forever. Our lives—filled as they are with the grief and suffering of existence on earth—seem intolerably long, but considering eternity, they are only a few breaths, a short tunnel passage on a long cross-country journey.

Because we are in a shadowy tunnel, we cannot see beyond the solid rock walls. One day we will emerge into the light and recognize that the tunnel was not the focus of the journey itself, it was simply a dark passage into the light and openness of day. From God's perspective, life on earth is as transitory as a car speeding through a mountain tunnel. For this reason, Jesus taught us to lay up treasures in Heaven rather than on earth (Matthew 6:19-21). The *Westminster Confession* approaches the issue somewhat differently by stating that the chief end of man is to glorify God and enjoy Him forever. The transitory, temporary lives God allotted to us on this planet are not the point in themselves. We were not created to make a name for ourselves, but to magnify the Lord of the universe.

Conversely, life at times seems as difficult to endure as breathlessness in the tunnel. Obtaining a comforting infusion of oxygen seems to be of more immediate importance than worshiping God. This is how the suffering of loss hits us. We are hurting. We are angry at God, who created us for Himself. Our need for recovery from the loss seems more immediately important than relationship with others.

Now consider Jesus on the cross. He was in the midst of suffering a hideously unjust sentence of death, deserted by friends, and seemingly deserted by the Father. Yet, even while dying on the cross, He did not cease to make Himself available to others. He provided for His mother, encouraged the thief hanging beside Him, and forgave His executioners. We could better understand someone self-centeredly focusing on the wounds inflicted unjustly. We could certainly understand this in the case of the suffering Jesus was forced to undergo. We would understand if He had called down imprecations on the entire human race for what we did to Him. Instead, He endured the suffering and forgave. Jesus demonstrates that *no wound is so deep that we are ever justified to refuse to love and give again.* Corrie Ten Boom, a Christian survivor of the Nazi death camps, affirmed this when she said, "No pit is so deep that God is not deeper still."

1. The "tunnel" is a picture of the brevity and difficulty of life in a world that is increasingly evil and hostile to the believer. What other pictures can you think of that convey an illustration about life in a sinful world?

2. In considering a loss you have experienced, describe your relationship with others who are with you in the tunnel.

3. After being wounded, we all have a tendency to guard and protect ourselves in such a way that we will never be hurt again. Giving to others often seems like too great a risk when we have been deeply hurt.

What do you think is the difference between the kind of giving demonstrated by the New Testament religious leaders, and the kind of giving and loving Jesus demonstrated? (See Luke 11:42, 21:1-4; Matthew 9:35-36.)

4. What are the risks involved when a Christian chooses to love and give as Jesus did?

THE SPHERES OF TECHNIQUES AND CYNICISM

The reality of the time we have on earth is that it is a short tunnel ride in relation to eternal life. We are involved in a program that is much, much bigger than ourselves. Introspection for the sake of introspection is fruitless because *we are not the point* of what God is doing. Still, we easily feel indignation because we remain in the tunnel. As we noted earlier in this guide, this kind of anger is understandable, even natural, because we were not created for loss, but for relationship with God and others. The danger of dwelling on this inevitable anger is that when we acknowledge our frustrations, we arrive at a crossroads where we must choose between two spheres.

We are using the word sphere in the sense of a domain of action or existence. In other words, a sphere is a place where we act out our view of life and the world. Most people are convinced, or perhaps hooked on the idea, that there is some key—a method, some steps, a universal set of principles—that will guarantee success or happiness. We call this the "technical sphere" because people are diligently searching for some technique or method that will make life work. Techniques are great for solving technical "problems": repairing the car, curing cancer, even getting an astronaut to the moon. Technical problems are problems that can be solved.

As great a technical accomplishment as landing on the moon was, most of us do not consider it to have much of an impact on our lives. At the risk of angering the scientific community, we might even call it trivial.

The really important issues have to do with relationships: our walk with God, longing to be recognized by our parents, encouraging a struggling believer. But relationships are messy, frustrating, and chaotic. As most of us are keenly aware, no steps or formulas can guarantee that our hearts will not break. Many of those brilliant men and women who helped Neil Armstrong step onto the lunar plain were more perplexed at their relationships with spouses, family, and friends than they ever were with their monumental technical task. Nevertheless, many of us approach relationships and grief the way a scientist approaches an experiment. We believe that if we come up with the right formula, then life will work, perhaps splendidly.

People who approach their relationships in the technical sphere often look to be in control on the outside, but are in despair and confusion on the inside. They are weary because of the unrelenting pursuit of deliverance, recovery, and escape from the pain of living in a sinful world.

But if we are to be honest about life, we must experience a brush with cynicism; walking through suffering is essential to genuine spiritual growth. We enter the *sphere of cynicism* when we recognize that the methods we have embraced to manage our lives have failed to produce the desired result. The goal may have been health, comfort, or avoidance of conflict. Yet life guarantees none of these things, even though we diet, exercise, mind our own business, treat others with kindness, and petition God, hoping to avoid the suffering of life.

We have known Christians who have prospered so

49

much and suffered so little that they either believe they are God's specially chosen ones, or they are convinced they have discovered principles that obligate God to answer their prayers. However, the bumps of life inevitably come. These "bumps" are really opportunities to give up our attempts to manage life apart from God and to depend on Him instead. It often takes time before we are able to see suffering as an opportunity to trust God. So, we are initially surprised and hurt when suffering touches us.

We have a friend who has been a surgeon for a number of years. In all that time he has performed many operations and has been privy to a good deal of human suffering. Sometimes the patient dies. Occasionally even a successful operation buys the patient only a short amount of time. He often has to break difficult news to family members. Once, a mother flew into hysteric convulsions when he told her that her son would be permanently paralyzed.

Not long ago, he said that he was angry at God for the first time in his life because his wife had been diagnosed with a terminal illness. Where had the doctor been all this time? Why did he fail to be touched by the enormous suffering that was all around him? The surgeon was required to take stock of the apparent vanity of life apart from God because he was personally touched by the effects of the Fall of humankind.

This is what we mean by the sphere of cynicism. When we are forced to conclude that the techniques we use to manage life comfortably (and thus manage God as well) are delusions, we enter the cynical sphere. We must admit that we cannot box God in, and we look at the world in a new way. We become dissatisfied with pat answers and critical of those who peddle simple solutions. This new way of looking at life can be a big step forward. Honesty about life often brings an exhilarating sense of freedom: "no more pretending," in spite of the possibility that my friends will worry about the change in me. To enter this sphere is very much like

50

the child who puts away toys for the final time: We will no longer entertain childish delusions that we can make life work.

When we are personally touched by suffering and loss we not only respond with rage and despair, but we also demonstrate our beliefs about God and life in a sinful world. In walking through the turbulent waters of our anger, doubts, and fears, we deeply discover God's promised presence and comfort. *The only way we will ever be available to love and give again is if we are willing to walk through the waters.*

This promise God made to Israel is a picture that can help us understand suffering:

> "When you pass through the waters,
>   I will be with you;
> and when you pass through the rivers,
>   they will not sweep over you.
> When you walk through the fire,
>   you will not be burned;
>   the flames will not set you ablaze."
> (Isaiah 43:2)

5. a. What do the water and fire threaten to do?

   b. What do we learn about God's perspective on suffering from this passage?

6. a. Why would the person in the technical sphere (as discussed earlier) resist walking through these kinds of waters?

51

b. What does their resistance reveal about their views of life and of God?

7. What kind of comfort might the person in the technical sphere give to another person who is suffering loss?

8. Read 2 Corinthians 1:3-7. What are some results of allowing ourselves to walk through the pain of our grief and feel the impact of our loss?

To come to the realization that we live and move in a world that is full to the brim of evil and suffering is a healthy sense of reality, but there is also a great danger. Comfort with cynicism can turn us into grasping, bitter, narcissistic loners. We cannot return to a Pollyanna-like denial; we must move on to the kind of *availability* Jesus demonstrated. We must have no delusions about the reality of life and human nature, but we must also love and give again. Honesty about the inadequacy of our techniques is not enough. Christian cynics are critical of the church, its leaders, other Christians, and the wisdom of the past. Rather than offer helpful suggestions and real comfort, cynics gather with other cynics to snipe at those who are not initiated into their cynicism. They divide churches, split families, and offer very little comfort to those who are suffering loss. In fact, the cynics we have known tend to avoid people who are going through suffering.

We have a friend who was very critical of the church. One of her criticisms was that the pastor's sermons did not contain enough references to the believer's position and identity in Christ. She continually quoted a particular seminar speaker who had opened a new world to her when he taught the importance of one's position in Christ. Evidently this truth had liberated her to face the questions of life realistically and in light of her position.

We were surprised when this woman seemed to be purposely avoiding us after a relative died several years ago. We received many expressions of sympathy and love from friends in our church community, but there was a conspicuous silence from this woman. Shortly after our loss we were at the grocery store and saw her at the opposite end of the aisle. She looked up, and a horrified expression appeared on her face when she recognized us. She quickly pushed her cart away, apparently hoping that we had not seen her. Her behavior puzzled us. Several months later she apologized. "I have this fear of grieving people," she said. "I'm just never sure what to say." How different she seemed as she made her admission. No longer was she the self-sufficient possessor of truth, however cynical.

9. With which of the two spheres (technical or cynical) do you more closely identify? Why?

10. How have you responded to grieving people in the past? (Have you avoided them, risked blundering, or been a source of comfort and encouragement?)

BEYOND DESPAIR AND CYNICISM

Our friend illustrates the tragedy of remaining in the cynical sphere. Cynicism is just another attempt to insulate us from the very suffering of life we are sure we understand so well. Cynics pride themselves on being honest. Honesty is a wonderful virtue, but it leaves us in a blind alley if we lose the sense that, though we are important to God, *we are not the point.*

53

Honestly facing disappointments must lead us to embrace the true God. He cannot be managed by the techniques of those who are in denial, and He also calls us to love and give — something the cynic will not bring himself to do.

The person in denial is really confused and in despair. Despair is our condition when our formulas to manage life don't work, but we stubbornly stick to them anyway. The despairing person is angry at God, at self, and at others, but buries it underneath a facade of methods, steps, formulas, and techniques. Something has to work; the alternative is terrifying. He uses formulas rather than worshiping God in truth. Because he is in denial he cannot love God and others.

The cynic is in a better position. He is under no delusions. He knows God cannot be managed by method. The problem is that the cynic gives up any effort to love God or others because he fears he cannot do it honestly. He has seen too much of life's suffering, and he is fed up with techniques. His hatred of technique is so strong that he becomes comfortable criticizing the "hypocrites" who cling to them. In doing this the cynic is denying the message of the gospel; he is not available to love God and to love others.

There is another alternative to despair and cynicism. As we have said, we are not the point. So, what is the point? We are part of a program that is being carried forward by an all-powerful God. Political news portrays that economics is the point. The playboy believes that sexual freedom is the point. Labor unions believe that workers' security is the point. But economics, sex, and security are just cracks in the wall of this tunnel we're passing through. God is the point.

Therefore, if our losses are to have any benefit to us, we must face the claims God makes on our lives. He calls us to love Him and to love others. We must move beyond denial and cynicism and toward *the sphere of availability*. Availability is not another technique. It is the result of accepting the claims God makes on us and choosing to worship Him, "the God of mystery," in the midst of a confusing world.

The emphasis is on availability because I can accept the claims God makes on me, even though life may be mixed with suffering, and still reach out to others. I am available to be used by Him.

Unlike the technical person, the available person struggles with the problem of suffering in the world but does not make escape from suffering the goal of life. No one permanently abides in the sphere of availability; there is a constant tension. The available person is "prone to wander."[1] Unlike the cynic, the available person is not smugly immobilized by the sinful, tainted motivations of people. To be available is to move courageously into others' lives in spite of the possibility of impure motives and the seeming absurdity all around us, because God's Word commands community and relationship with other believers.

What does this discussion about "three spheres" have to do with loss? No one can completely prepare to receive suffering and loss, but suffering and loss can prepare us to face the realities of living in a sinful world. Embracing loss changes us forever, but we must not allow it to immobilize us permanently. Jesus demonstrated complete availability on the cross, helping the griever grasp that *no wound is so deep that we are ever justified to refuse to love and give again.* This truth does not negate the fact that comforters must give grievers time and space to work through their loss in an appropriate way. There are too many stories of gross insensitivity on the part of comforters. We've all heard accounts of the insensitivity of Christians toward those in the grief process. The decision to love and give again should be made by the griever who has benefited from a community environment of careful nurture and gentle encouragement. At best, one who is forced to "get on with life" before he or she is ready will relate only limply and without passion to others.

The next session will deal with the courage that is needed to continue to worship God and comfort others after suffering loss.

11. Read Philippians 1:12-26 and 2 Timothy 4:8-18.
    What observations would you make about how Paul
    handled his woundedness?

12. In what ways have others in your Christian com-
    munity effectively encouraged you to love and give
    again after your loss?

STILLNESS

Lord Jesus, it seems absurd to give and love again
without a guarantee that I will escape suffering.
It is easier for me to . . . than to risk the wounds
of suffering in love. Your Word and Your action
on the cross silence my most reasonable excuses
never to love and give again. What I fear the most
about loving and giving is. . . .

DURING THE WEEK

Read back through the text in this session. What issues
especially stand out to you as meaningful? Take some
time to journal on the thoughts and feelings you have.

NOTE
 1. Robert Robinson (1735–1790), "Come, Thou Fount of Every Blessing."

THE COURAGE TO COMFORT

ૐ

It was a beautiful, serene country cemetery surrounded by lush green fields, which suggested life in spite of the flowerpots and marble statues that reminded of death and decay. I (Precious) sat quietly beside my friend on a stone bench next to the new mound of earth beneath which her mother's body lay. At first she shared tears and memories, but then came silence. During this stony silence, I was screaming on the inside because of how impotent I felt. I groped for profoundly wise words that might bring comfort to her. I so wanted to say something that would relieve her. Instead, I intruded into her moment of grief. I could hardly believe my ears as the air filled with empty and predictable chatter that was calculated to comfort not my friend, but me.

That evening I felt self-condemning emotions. At first I told myself, *You know better than that.* Then my flagellation turned to a sense of sorrow for my own arrogance in directing all my energies to my own comfort, and leaving a friend without comfort on her bench of mourning. I had always read with disquiet and condemnation the accounts in the Old Testament of Job's friends only adding grief when he was troubled and sorrowful. Yet that night I saw myself as a modern Eliphaz, Bildad, or Zophar, lacking not theological truth, but the courage to remain

in the sacred silence of a friend who was overcome
by grief.

A DESIRE TO COMFORT

Both comforters and grievers sense powerlessness and
impotence in association with the grief process. In grief
we are confronted with circumstances beyond our control and even our ability to explain. We feel confusing
emotions when we must evaluate the meaning of our
loss against the backdrop of our present world. We
know grief's familiar face when we see it, but no two
grievers experience it in the same way. The unique
fingerprint of grief impresses feelings of aloneness on
the griever just at the time when the need for someone
is the greatest. Comforters who too quickly attempt to
divert the attention of the bereaved to past memories,
future potentials, or heavenly scenes isolate rather than
comfort.

1. Gethsemane was a place where Christ walked
   through His agony. Read Matthew 26:36-46, and
   answer the following questions.

   a. What did Christ want from His disciples?

   b. How did they respond to His need?

   c. What does Gethsemane teach us about grieving?

d. How have you responded to those who have "fallen asleep" at the moment of your agony?

Jesus' action on the cross displays forgiveness without denying the reality of the wrong that was done. Gethsemane is a picture of Christ's agony over sin and His passion to offer forgiveness to those who do not even see their need. We feel pain when friends "fall asleep" during our time of anguish. It is easier either to minimize the wrong done or to be engulfed with bitterness and resentment than to offer forgiveness without denying the wrong that was done.

2. a. In what ways has your grief made you feel lonely and isolated?

b. What do you want most at those moments?

c. How do you usually handle these feelings?

d. What would most communicate comfort to you?

What do we need to understand if we have a desire to comfort others? Mainly, there is nothing wrong with wanting to be a comforter. Most people can recall something clumsy they said in the presence of someone who was grieving. If you attempt to comfort others, you will blow it from time to time. What the bereaved will remember is your heart.

THE HEART OF THE COMFORTER

A number of years ago I (Precious) spent five months in the hospital with a life-threatening illness. An emergency surgery was performed, which even though successful, left the future in doubt for me. I not only grieved because of the way the surgery had intruded in my life, I was also filled with fears about the future. In those dark hours my family stayed by my side and many friends visited, prayed, and sent cards with words of encouragement. During that time, my faith and hope felt so fragile. In my suffering I observed three different types of comforters. On the basis of my observations, I concluded that we are prone to comfort for our own comfort's sake rather than being available for the sake of the sufferer.

The first category is the *fix-it comforter*. This person thinks that looking on the bright side, being positive, or adopting a fighting attitude will make things right. Positive mental attitudes are not bad in themselves, but such attitudes can be inappropriately used as a demand that God fix the problem (when He has the right to allow the problem to run its course), or as an insulating blanket from reality. Sometimes the fix-it comforter is terrified for himself. He desperately wants the griever's problem to be fixed because he worries for his stable view of life if it is not.

A flock of these comforters marched into and out of my hospital room. One young man brought his guitar and asked if there was any sin I had failed to confess. Another man pleaded with me to memorize Psalm 51 and repeat it over and over. A doctor's wife told me that God would certainly heal me, I just needed more faith. A pastor stood at the foot of my bed and preached a sermon as if he were speaking to 500 instead of just to me. I felt sadness for these comforters because I came to realize that they were really seeking comfort from me, and in the midst of suffering I had little comfort to give them.

The second category is the *define-it comforter*. This person is also trapped. He wants to sit with the griever and dream of reasons why God is putting you through this. He wants a definition of what the griever is learning through the experience.

In the define-it comforter, I didn't sense a heart that really wanted to comfort me, and he couldn't handle what I was really learning through my experience. What I was really learning was that no one understood my grief, that Heaven is silent, and that there is no scriptural guarantee that I would ever leave the hospital alive. So, if I told the comfortor in this category anything, I told him what I thought he wanted to hear.

The third category of comforter is *loving and giving*. These comforters taught me what it means to comfort others. This is the kind of comforter I wanted to be to my friend in the cemetery.

Late one night in the hospital I could not sleep. I was dreading another sleepless night with physical pain and the uncertainty that I would even be alive in the morning. There was one night nurse who seemed to be particularly kind when she visited my room. I realized how busy she must be with the large number of patients on that wing, but I took a risk in asking her to sit with me awhile. To my surprise, she agreed. She took my hand and sat silently in the chair for what seemed like an hour—at least until I fell asleep. She said nothing profound—indeed, she said nothing at all—but she effectively comforted me. My fears slowly faded, and I was able to rest.

Another night, the elders of the church came to my hospital room and prayed for my healing. These are rugged, hardworking men who have known me all my life. They tenderly offered their prayers with tears as they passionately approached God's throne of grace on my behalf. It was a scene of compassion I will never forget.

Grievers are lonely people who want comforters who can endure the uncomfortable silence. Job's three friends were effective comforters for seven days (Job 2:13). But after they opened their mouths, God declared His counsel had been darkened "with words without knowledge" (Job 38:2). A knowledge of the well-documented "stages of grief" is helpful, but comforters can be helpful if they remember to be patient and quiet. To be silent takes great courage because the comforter will find that something is happening within him or her while sitting beside the one who has endured the loss. We can hope that one conclusion the comforter will draw is that grief is inconsolable.

3. a. What kind of comforters did you encounter in the midst of your own loss?

   b. What did the comforters do or say that meant the most to you? (*Option:* Call or write that special comforter and let him or her know what this meant to you.)

4. Why do you think those who are experiencing loss seem to value "presence but quietness"?

WHY IS GRIEF INCONSOLABLE?

When I sat with my friend in the cemetery, I was uncomfortable with her silence. But I had a genuine desire to bring comfort to her as well as an agenda to be comfortable. I was mistaken to think that I could offer words or actions that would lessen her grief. In fact, to think that I could make it better was presumptuous. There are at least three reasons for this.

Grief is a here-and-now pain. Verbal attempts to comfort often focus on future possibilities or the reality of another dimension for the griever. How else would one comfort someone who has lost a loved one other than by offering the real hope of Heaven for the beloved, future possibilities of reunion, or a sensible reason to explain the loss? The problem is not that these perspectives are not the truth, but that they are often poorly timed. The griever usually needs to work through the present implications of the loss in this moment. And, in this moment, Heaven seems very far away and the pain of loss seems very real. The here-and-now pain also underscores what would really bring comfort but cannot be supplied.

5. Read Job 10. In this chapter, Job is experiencing the here-and-now pain of his grief.

a. What are some of the emotions Job expresses?

b. How does he seem to feel about life and God?

c. Which of Job's thoughts and emotions can you most identify with?

The relationship with the one lost cannot be restored, thus the griever can never return to life the way it was before. In a sense, there is no "getting back to normal," although the griever should eventually arrive at the point of putting the person who was lost into an important place of remembrance. The time required to arrive at that point varies greatly from griever to griever. The only thing that would take away the here-and-now pain of grief is restoration of the beloved in this moment. Although that type of comfort resulted when Jesus restored Lazarus to life (John 11:17-44), special resurrection is not our normative experience. But resurrection does provide a third reason that present grief is inconsolable.

Only God can provide true and lasting comfort. Jesus said, "Blessed are those who mourn, for they will be comforted" (Matthew 5:4). This leaves us questioning, Who will do the comforting, and when will they be comforted? Some think Jesus was referring to the comfort provided by sympathetic friends as God's agents during the grieving process. Such an interpretation is unlikely based on the context.

The Beatitudes, of which this verse is a part, are an address to those who have a righteousness which exceeds that of the religious leaders. The promises of inheriting the earth, seeing God, obtaining a Kingdom, and receiving a reward in Heaven indicate rewards that only God will bestow in the future, in eternity. The reason we cannot provide full consolation to the grieving is because genuine consolation awaits a future day. At that time, God will restore believers to each other — the beloved to the mourners. The mourners will feel much like the women in the days of Elijah and Elisha who "received back their dead, raised to life again" (Hebrews 11:35). However, unlike the consolation those women experienced, in the future resurrection the beloved will never again depart. This also demonstrates that for the believer much of grief is a longing for the time when death will be no more.

6. Many people are uncomfortable with the idea of a future hope because it does not seem to relate to their here-and-now pain. It often seems so "pie in the sky" with no present relevance. What are some

positive and negative reasons why many people are not interested in a future hope?

7. Read Revelation 21:3-4 (printed on page 41 of session 3). What comfort does this passage give to you in the here and now of your grief?

8. There is a saying, "You can't go home again." Grief changes lives in such a way that this saying is especially true in the life of someone who has experienced a loss. What are ways that your world is very different since your loss?

> LEADER: Guide the group in spending some time in prayer for one another and for others who are experiencing loss.

STILLNESS

You may want to have a time of praise and thanksgiving for what God has done for you through the Lord Jesus Christ. You may also want to thank Him for those who have brought you "tastes of Heaven" in the midst of your loss. It would be appropriate to pray for one another, that God might use the things you have learned to make you available to Him and a genuine comfort to others.

DURING THE WEEK

We often feel like questioning God's goodness as we experience the deeply felt consequences of life in an imperfect world. Yet we cannot define God's goodness in such a way that demands He spare us the consequences of sin. We are sinners, and the wages of sin is death (Romans 3:23). Yet God's goodness is clearly seen in the free gift of eternal life He offers to us (6:23). The full realizations of eternal life, Heaven, and the Kingdom are part of the "not yet" tension we must live with presently.

- In what ways has your understanding of God's goodness in the past left you puzzled when bad things happened?

- If you struggle with God's goodness in the here and now, put words to your struggle in a journal, a letter to God, or prayer before His throne of grace.

- Read Psalm 73 and observe the psalmist's struggle with God's goodness. In what ways do you identify with what the psalmist expresses?

COURAGE TO MEET THE SUFFERING GOD

&

Only God can provide lasting consolation. Still, what is God doing presently in our grief? Answering this question properly should cause us to worship Him. Unfortunately, some grievers go beyond a natural anger directed toward God and embrace a bitterness that holds God to be culpable for the loss.

BELIEVING GOD IN THE MIDST OF TENSION

In an effort to avoid admitting that God is mysterious and cannot be controlled, some people have tried to explain suffering. They claim they merely want harmony and reduced tension. In reality, the harmonization is motivated by a sinful desire to control and regulate God, removing all mystery from Him.

One sinister attempt to explain suffering in this world and God's role in it is to *view God as a victim.* The proponents of this view see God as loving and compassionate, weeping with us in our suffering, yet powerless to intervene in the face of tragedy. They believe that bad things happen to good people because God is not really all-powerful. They would no doubt be disappointed to learn that no such god exists.

We find greater comfort trusting in the mysterious purposes of an all-powerful, just God who does not suspend suffering than in a wimpy god who wrings his hands when another tragedy happens because he can't stop it. At least the all-powerful God has a benevolent purpose. He will bring good from evil. If the wimpy god is thwarted by evil now, if evil has not only *apparently* won, but has *actually* won in the present, then good can never be recovered from present tragedies. The Bible describes a God of mystery who allows suffering He could halt at any time, but chooses not to for only generally disclosed reasons. He promises that these reasons will be made clear to all creatures in the future. *The God of the Bible is all-powerful.*

Another view meant to promote harmony is that God is an *agent* rather than a victim. God in this view is a cosmic sadist. He is certainly all-powerful, but he turns his back on his suffering creatures. The deists of the Enlightenment were committed to this view of suffering, but they are by no means the only advocates of this view. Some advocates are peppered throughout evangelical churches. These people are quick to quote Romans 8:28 (out of context) to dismiss and seal hermetically the wound of the confused, questioning mourner: "What's the problem? (God has a perfect right to take your teenage son.) He'll work it for good . . . you'll see." Otherwise theologically orthodox, these functioning deists are terrible comforters because they have no concept of the great heart and compassion of God. *The God of the Bible is loving and compassionate.*

When we examine Scripture we indeed see an all-powerful God who with a word brings forth galaxies, destroys empires, and calms the raging storms. Yet within the same written text we are confronted with the God-Man Jesus, who exalts children and weeps with friends beside a tomb He intends to open. To believe in a compassionate, loving God who is all-powerful leaves us with a terrifying silence as a temporary answer to our "why" questions and forces us to ask ourselves, "Can we trust this God, who embodies the very essence of love, with the most disturbing doubts that result from tragic circumstances that at first glance seem to declare His impotence?"

The tension created by our attempts to know an all-powerful but loving God brings us to One who compares Himself to the untameable leviathan (Job 41:1). Nicholas Wolterstorff spoke about his own struggle when faced with this mysterious God:

> I cannot fit it all together by saying, "He did it," but neither can I do so by saying, "There was nothing he could do about it."
>
> I cannot fit it together at all. I can only, with Job, endure. I do not know why God did not prevent Eric's death. To live without the answer is precarious. It's hard to keep one's footing.[1]

The result of God's face-to-face talk with Job is the sufferer's repentance. The struggle with a loving and all-powerful God should lead us to repentance, worship, and . . . hope.

1. a. What are some examples of the hard questions you asked of God in the midst of your loss?

   b. How have you have handled the tensions raised by these hard questions?

2. a. In what ways has your view of God changed since you experienced your loss?

   b. How has this change affected your grief?

THERE IS HOPE

Grievers desperately need hope. They keenly feel that God has left them here, but for what purpose? Is there any hope, and what does it look like? In pain we often settle for something far less than the hope with which God intended to comfort us. We opt for relief and recovery in another how-to book, another group, another seminar, another answer to the plight of suffering humanity, in the same way a desert traveler drags himself toward a mirage. We are thirsty and weary travelers in what Swiss philosopher Max Picard called a "flight from God." We're often content with mirages when He offers springs of living water, with crumbs when He promises a feast.

However, it is the *path* to the spring that we fear the most. The path goes by the way of the cross, and there we must meet suffering. We must look upon Jesus, the Man of sorrows, and not turn away from His penetrating gaze that sees clearly into our hearts, which are determined to make life work apart from Him. He sees our fierce rage at being placed in a cold, dark tunnel with yawning cracks that threaten to cave in, when instead we were created for the warmth of sunshine and the bounty of a garden.

At the cross we meet two criminals, suffering the deserved consequences for their actions (Luke 23:33, 39-43). The words of the criminals give a picture of two responses to living in a sinful world. One refuses to yield to God's claims, but instead shouts, "Aren't you the Christ? Save yourself and us!" (verse 39) — spare us this painful consequence of sin. If You are truly God, then the most effective way to prove Your power and love is to spare us the consequences. The unrepentant man arrogantly raged at God for allowing him to be touched by the results of sin. He deserved death, yet to the bitter end he demanded that God spare him.

In contrast, the other thief is irresistibly drawn to look upon the wounds of the dying Christ. This man sees himself as the Savior's executioner and accepts the justice of his own end. He sees the wounds inflicted on this innocent Man as deeper than any wounds he himself bore. With a heart that can no longer remain untouched and hardened, he pleads for mercy and forgiveness, and asks to be remembered in the Kingdom. Jesus, honoring his repentant heart, remembers him. We come to understand suffering when we see that no wound is greater than Christ's wound, inflicted by a sin-ridden humanity.

But our journey does not leave us on a rugged hilltop. It takes us on to a garden of life, of hope, of death conquered, and a new day promised. We see the resurrected Savior who provides us with hope, though we are not yet in that day. What does this hope look like? Those who have this hope grieve losses fully: They are outraged by injustice, anguish with deeply felt heaves of sorrow, and weep beside new graves. This hope has tastes of the new day, which are provided by a good God who has surrounded us with reminders of Himself. Creation mirrors the effects of the Fall, but the glory of God is evident as well. The glory of creation with its tastes of God's new day creates a thirst that is unquenchable in those who refuse to settle for a mirage, but instead choose to struggle and to give cups of cold water to those who thirst (Matthew 10:42).

People of hope have the courage to sit in silence on your bench of mourning. People of hope have ears to listen to stories of abuse and abandonment. People of hope believe that God will keep His promises of resurrection, restoration, and glorification in the future. They cling to God's goodness, which will be fully tasted on that day when death, pain, and loss will be captured and forever destroyed. "They are longing for a better country — a heavenly one" (Hebrews 11:16). They are thus *available* to God and to others around them, because they are familiar with grief.

We must choose to allow grief to change our lives and make us people of hope who are available to comfort and encourage. Nicholas Wolterstorff commented on the power of grief to change our lives forever:

71

To believe in Christ's rising and death's dying is also to live with the power and the challenge to rise up now from all our dark graves of suffering love. If sympathy for the world's wounds is not enlarged by our anguish, if love for those around us is not expanded, if gratitude for what is good does not flame up, if insight is not deepened, if commitment to what is important is not strengthened, if aching for a new day is not intensified, if hope is weakened and faith diminished, if from the experience of death comes nothing good, then death has won. Then death, be proud.[2]

Finally, people of hope laugh, love, and experience the beauty of the setting sun. For this hope knows that these too are gifts from God, and our enjoyment of what He gives to us is a vital part of worshiping Him as the Creator. So there are flowers to plant, songs to write, pictures to paint, and children to hold, especially as we ride through the tunnel together.

Look, children, we are almost out of the tunnel.

LEADER: If the participants have already read Hebrews 11 before the group meeting, just read verses 13-16,39-40 again together.

---

3. Read Hebrews 11.

 a. What important admission or confession is made by the person whose life is characterized by faith?

b. What is the disappointment of the person of faith?

c. What longing and eventual reward make the person of faith also a person of hope?

An element of worship is to so enter into the fellowship of Jesus' suffering for a world that chose to be independent of Him that I taste of His sorrow for my sin. I will then glimpse the goodness He lavishes on me daily through creation, the Bible, and people who mirror His image. My enjoyment of these remnants delights Him because He created them for my enjoyment and His glory. To refuse to experience pleasure, to create, to discover beauty is refusal to worship Him. His heart must grieve as He prepares an indescribable banquet table at which we may feast, yet we seem content with bread crumbs.

4. a. Read Isaiah 61:1-3. What does this passage teach us about grief and worship?

b. What would be required if you were to adorn yourself with a "crown of beauty" and a "garment of praise"?

c. How can your grief display God's splendor?

STILLNESS

Take time to praise the Lord for what He has begun in your life through this study. Change often seems to be slow, and you may not feel you are where you wanted to be by the end of this study. Thank Him for His unrelenting pursuit of you and His grace that indeed is irresistible. Thank Him for His goodness that promises a coming day when your pain from . . . will be forever silenced.

DURING THE WEEK

Share your story of grief with someone in the group. What are some common themes or motifs in your story? Would you tell your story differently than you did in session 1?

NOTES
  1. Nicholas Wolterstorff, *Lament for a Son* (Grand Rapids, MI: Eerdmans, 1987), page 67.
  2. Wolterstorff, page 92.

HELP FOR LEADERS

ะ

This guide is ideal in a group of four to twelve people.
Because God has designed Christians to function as a
body, we learn and grow more when we interact with
others than we would on our own. If you are on your
own, see if you can recruit a few other people to join
you in working through this guide. You can use the
guide on your own, but you'll probably long for someone to talk with about it. On the other hand, if you have
a group larger than twelve we suggest that you divide
into smaller groups of six or so for discussion. With
more than twelve people, you begin to move into a large
group dynamic, and not everyone has the opportunity
to participate.

The following pages are designed to help a discussion leader guide the group in an edifying time
centered on God's truth and grace. You may want one
appointed person to lead all the sessions, or you may
want to rotate leadership.

PREPARATION

Your aim as a leader is to create an environment that
encourages people to feel safe enough to be honest
with themselves, the group, and God. Group members
should sense that no question is too dumb to ask, that

the other participants will care about them no matter what they reveal about themselves, and that each person's opinion is as valid as everyone else's. At the same time, they should know that the Bible is your final authority for what is true.

As the group leader, your most important preparation for each session is prayer. You will want to make your prayers personal, of course, but here are some suggestions:

- Pray that group members will be able to attend the discussion consistently. Ask God to enable them to feel safe enough to share vulnerable thoughts and feelings honestly, and to contribute their unique gifts and insights.

- Pray for group members' private times with God. Ask Him to be active in nurturing each person.

- Ask the Holy Spirit for guidance in exercising patience, acceptance, sensitivity, and wisdom. Pray for an atmosphere of genuine love in the group, with each member being honestly open to learning and change.

- Pray that your discussion will lead each of you to obey the Lord more closely and demonstrate His presence to others.

- Pray for insight and wisdom as you lead the group.

After prayer, your most important preparation is to be thoroughly familiar with the material you will discuss. Before each meeting, be sure to read the text and answer all of the questions for yourself. This will prepare you to think ahead of questions group members might raise.

Choose a time and place to meet that is consistent, comfortable, and relatively free from distractions. Refreshments can help people mingle, but don't let this consume your study and discussion time.

LEADING THE GROUP

As you conduct each session keep the following in mind.

Work toward a safe, relaxed, and open atmosphere. This may not come quickly, so as the leader you must model acceptance, humility, openness to truth and change, and love. Develop a genuine interest in each person's remarks, and expect to learn from them. Show that you care by listening carefully. Be affirming and sincere. Sometimes a hug is the best response — sometimes a warm silence is.

You may need to ask a warm-up question. Group members will be coming to sessions with their minds full of the events of the day. To help them start thinking about the topic at hand, it is sometimes helpful to begin the session with a warm-up question. You may want to ask group members to talk briefly about what they have observed about themselves during the previous week as related to the study's topic. This type of opening discussion early in the group process invites participants to let the others get to know them better.

Pay attention to how you ask questions. By your tone of voice, convey your interest in and enthusiasm for the question and your warmth toward the group. The group members will adopt your attitude. Read the questions as though you were asking them of good friends.

If the discussion falters, keep these suggestions in mind:

- Be comfortable with silence. Let the group wrestle to think of answers. Some of the questions require thought or reflection on one's life. Don't be quick to jump in and rescue the group with your answers.

- On the other hand, you should answer questions yourself occasionally. In particular, you should be the first to answer questions about personal experiences. In this way you will model the depth of vulnerability you hope others will show. Count on this: If you are open, others will be too, and vice versa. Don't answer every question, but don't be a silent observer.

■ Reword a question if you perceive that the group has trouble understanding it as written.

■ If a question evokes little response, feel free to leave it and move on.

■ When discussion is winding down on a question, go on to the next one. It's not necessary to push people to see every angle.

Ask only one question at a time. Often, participants' responses will suggest a follow-up question to you. Be discerning as to when you are following a fruitful train of thought and when you are going on a tangent.

Be aware of time. It's important to honor the commitment to end at a set time.

Encourage constructive controversy. The group members can learn a great deal from struggling with the many sides of an issue. If you aren't threatened when someone disagrees, the whole group will be more open and vulnerable. Intervene when necessary, making sure that people debate ideas and interpretations, not attack each others' feelings or character. If the group gets stuck in an irreconcilable argument, say something like, "We can agree to disagree here," and move on.

Encourage autonomy with the group members. With a beginning group, you may have to ask all the questions and do all the planning. But within a few meetings you should start delegating various leadership tasks. Help members learn to exercise their gifts. Let them start making decisions and solving problems together. Encourage them to maturity and unity in Christ.

Validate both feelings and objective facts. Underneath the umbrella of Scripture, there is room for

78

both. People's feelings are often a road map to a biblical truth they need, but truth takes time to sink in. Expressing feelings—even negative ones like anger and fear—helps a person become more able not to be controlled by them. Give group members permission to feel things they wouldn't feel if they totally understood and trusted God. But of course, participants are responsible to express feelings in ways that don't dominate the group or damage others.

Summarize the discussion. Summarizing what has been said will help the group members see where the discussion is going and keep them more focused.

Don't feel compelled to "finish." It would be easy to spend an entire session on one or two questions. As leader, you will be responsible to decide when to cut off one discussion and move to another question, and when to let a discussion go on even though you won't have time for some questions. There will almost certainly be more questions than you need because we want you to be able to select those that seem most helpful for your unique group. Throughout this guide you'll find suggestions for selecting among questions.

Let the group plan applications. The ideas in the "During the Week" section are suggestions. Your group should adapt them to be relevant and life-changing for the members. If people see a genuine need that an application addresses, they are more likely to follow up. Help them see the connection between need and application.

End with refreshments. This gives people an excuse to stay for a few extra minutes and discuss the subject informally. Often the most important conversations occur after the formal session.

DURING THE FIRST SESSION

You or someone else in the group can open the session with a short prayer dedicating your time to God.

It is significant how much more productive and honest a discussion is if the participants know each other. Some of the questions in this session are designed to help participants get acquainted. You can set an example of appropriate disclosure by being the first to answer some questions. Participants will be looking to you to let them know how much honesty is safe in this group. If you reveal your worst secrets in the first session, you may scare some participants away. Conversely, if you conceal anything that might make you look bad, participants will get the message that honesty isn't safe.

At some point during the session, go over the following guidelines. They will help make your discussion more fruitful, especially when you're dealing with issues that truly matter to people.

Confidentiality. No one should repeat what someone shares in the group unless that person gives permission. Even then, discretion is imperative. Be trustworthy. Participants should talk about their own feelings and experiences, not those of others.

Attendance. Each session builds on previous ones, and you need continuity with each other. Ask group members to commit to attending all six sessions unless an emergency arises.

Participation. This is a *group* discussion, not a lecture. It is important that each person participates in the group.

Honesty. Appropriate openness is a key to a good group. Be who you really are, not who you think you should be. On the other hand, don't reveal inappropriate details of your life simply for the shock value. The goal is relationship.